Parent's Introduction

Whether your child is a beginning reader, a reluctant reader, or an eager reader, this book offers a fun and easy way to encourage and help your child in reading.

Developed with reading education specialists, *We Both Read* books invite you and your child to take turns reading aloud. You read the left-hand pages of the book, and your child reads the right-hand pages—which have been written at one of six early reading levels. The result is a wonderful new reading experience and faster reading development!

You may find it helpful to read the entire book aloud yourself the first time, then invite your child to participate the second time. As you read, try to make the story come alive by reading with expression. This will help to model good fluency. It will also be helpful to stop at various points to discuss what you are reading. This will help increase your child's understanding of what is being read.

In some books, a few challenging words are introduced in the parent's text, distinguished with **bold** lettering. Pointing out and discussing these words can help to build your child's reading vocabulary. If your child is a beginning reader, it may be helpful to run a finger under the text as each of you reads. Please also notice that a "talking parent" ☺ icon precedes the parent's text, and a "talking child" ☺ icon precedes the child's text.

If your child struggles with a word, you can encourage "sounding it out," but keep in mind that not all words can be sounded out. Your child might pick up clues about a word from the picture, other words in the sentence, or any rhyming patterns. If your child struggles with a word for more than five seconds, it is usually best to simply say the word.

Most of all, remember to praise your child's efforts and keep the reading fun. After you have finished the book, ask a few questions and discuss what you have read together. Rereading this book multiple times may also be helpful for your child.

Try to keep the tips above in mind as you read together, but don't worry about doing everything right. Simply sharing the enjoyment of reading together will increase your child's reading skills and help to start your child off on a lifetime of reading enjoyment!

Big Cats,
Little Cats

A We Both Read® Book

Text Copyright © 2010, 2015 by Treasure Bay, Inc.

By Sindy McKay

Reading Consultant: Bruce Johnson, M.Ed.

This book is based in part on a We Read Phonics book, *Big Cats*, but it has been significantly expanded and adapted for the We Both Read shared-reading format. You may find the We Read Phonics version to be a complementary and helpful companion to this title.

We Both Read® is a trademark of Treasure Bay, Inc.

Published by
Treasure Bay, Inc.
P.O. Box 119
Novato, CA 94948 USA

Printed in Singapore

Library of Congress Catalog Card Number: 2014944095

ISBN: 978-1-60115-276-3

We Both Read® Books
Patent No. 5,957,693

Visit us online at:
www.TreasureBayBooks.com

PR -11-14

WE BOTH READ®

Big Cats, Little Cats

By Sindy McKay

TREASURE BAY

What's soft and furry and sometimes purrs?

A cat.

👓 Cats can be little. Cats can also be very . . .

 . . . big!

The tiger is the largest cat in the animal world, even bigger than a lion! A baby tiger is called . . .

. . . a cub.

Most tigers are orange. Some tigers are white. All tigers have stripes that are . . .

. . . black.

👀 Can you pet this cat?

No!

This big cat is called a *cheetah*. Its fur is tan with round black . . .

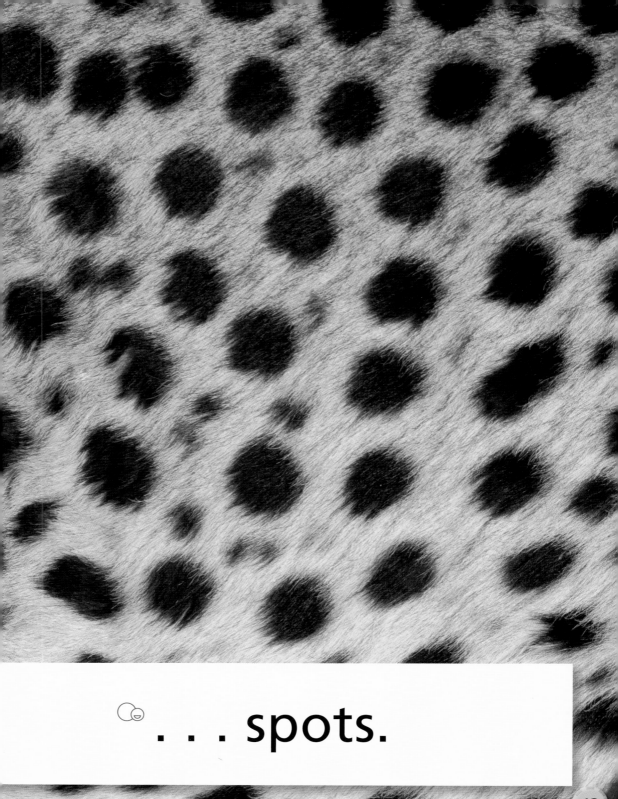

. . . spots.

👓 The cheetah can run faster than any other land animal.

Go, cat, go!

 Can you pet this cat?

No!

The lion is called the "king of the jungle." But sometimes even a king has to take . . .

. . . a nap.

How many lions do you see in this picture?

 Five!

A male lion has a growth of long hair around his neck called a *mane*. Female lions . . .

. . . do not.

 Can you pet these cats?

No!

Another big cat with spots on its fur is the leopard. Leopards are good climbers and often like to hang out in . . .

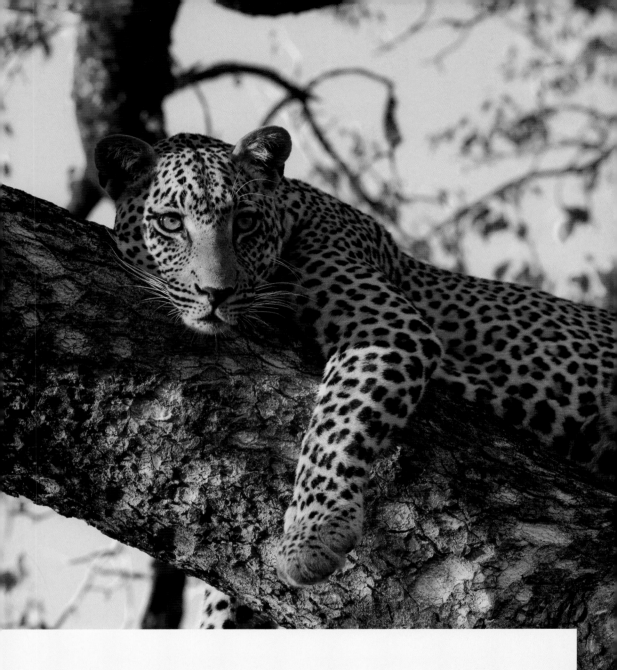

. . . trees.

A cat that looks similar to the leopard is called a *jaguar*. Many jaguars live in the rain forest, and they are very good swimmers. They like the . . .

. . . water.

Can you pet this cat?

No!

A cat that is sometimes called a *black panther* is actually a leopard whose fur is black. If you look closely, you can see . . .

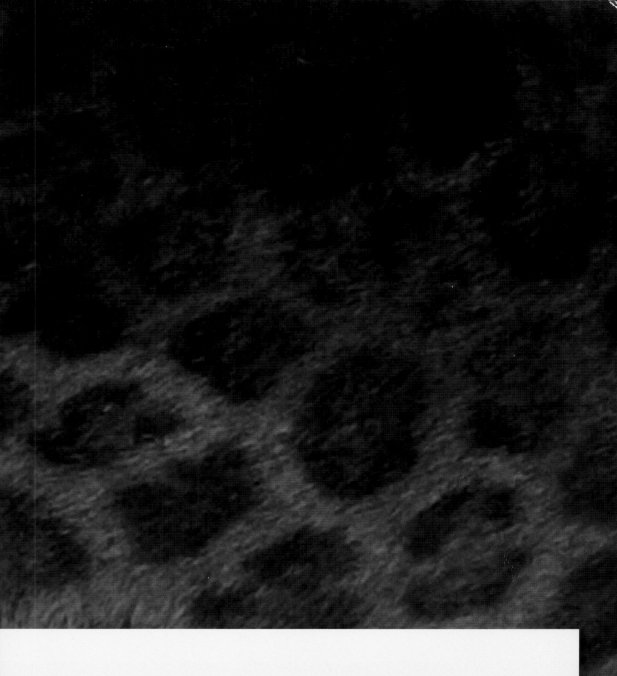

 . . . its spots.

Black panthers hunt at night when they are hard to see. During the day they often climb trees . . .

 . . . to rest.

 Can you pet this cat?

No!

Tigers, cheetahs, lions, jaguars, and leopards are relatives of the smaller furry pets found in many homes. They're all called . . .

. . . cats.

Can you pet this cat?

🗨 YES!

If you liked **Big Cats, Little Cats**, here is another
We Both Read® book you are sure to enjoy!

Museum Day

This book follows a young girl and her dad as they spend a charming day exploring all the fascinating exhibits in a museum. Along the way, a little bird adds some delightful humor as it manages to get into the museum and follows the girl and her dad throughout their day.

To see all the We Both Read books that are available,
just go online to **www.WeBothRead.com**.